Art History

Cinthia Milner

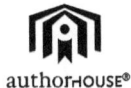

authorHOUSE®

AuthorHouse™
1663 Liberty Drive, Suite 200
Bloomington, IN 47403
www.authorhouse.com
Phone: 1-800-839-8640

First published by AuthorHouse 5/1/2008

ISBN: 978-1-4259-9019-0 (sc)

Library of Congress Control Number: 2008903774

Printed in the United States of America
Bloomington, Indiana

This book is printed on acid-free paper.

**To my mother, Frankie Ann Owen Milner,
with love, respect and thanksgiving.**

Joshua 4:19 On the tenth day of the first month the people went up from the Jordan and camped at Gilgal on the eastern border of Jericho.

Swimming

I swam before I walked. Early each morning, I jumped out of bed and ran to the water. I was so thrilled with another day, that I didn't notice the sharp rocks that scraped against my bare feet. I swam fast—deep strokes across the lake—and raced the sun as it climbed up from the backside of the mountains to give light to another day. I swam—panting, and pushing myself to beat the sun again. Then I sat on the opposite shore while the sun made its final climb. I watched as pink rays shot through the morning's fog, exhausted, catching my breath, and waited for that full blaze of heat before I swam back, shivering, and happy.

The Gift of Childhood

My childhood was my parents' gift to me. Very early in life, I knew myself, alone and quiet with only the sounds of an icy creek to keep me company, or the wind, or the call of a bird to break the silence. I marveled at everything, as I sat among the laurels and the lady slippers, so completely at home, I could have been one of them growing there.

No one had told me as yet to be accommodating, pleasing, sweet, and quiet. That came later and mostly from the men in my life. From them, I learned silence—not the silence of myself, that deep quiet place inside that was so familiar and loved by me, but the *silencing* of me—the loss of my very own voice, my very own words.

As that child, still protected, held back from the world by loving parents, I was still, simply, Ivy Nation. I was glorious, excited, unafraid and determined. For what, I didn't know. My life, I suppose, as any young girl should be and has a right to be.

My Young Lover

My young lover was exquisite. He was like an exotic bird. He had blue-black hair, green eyes, dark skin, and a large, beautifully sculpted body. He was handsome and wonderful to see, standing on the shore of the lake, glistening in the sunlight. The deepness of the colors I saw in his eyes as his adolescent storms passed through them, I believed to be the colors of a rain forest. The passion we shared took me beyond the soft, soothing colors of my home, and into the colors of a tropical paradise—with red so rich it dripped blood, and greens so deep and so vast, that I was left breathless, and drenched with sweat.

It was summer and it was hot. We made love everywhere. Water was our medium. My body, his body, the water—three made one. Water taught me lovemaking as it had taught me movement and physical strength—enveloping, surrendering, sinking, stretching out, floating, and caressing. In the arms of my lover, I felt the same as I had always felt in the depths of the lake.

Making Love

Making love came easily and naturally for me. I was happy with my body. I loved the feel of my chest as it rose and fell with my breath. I loved my arms, which were slender and tanned. I loved the shape of my feet and legs, the flatness of my stomach, and the small of my back. It was not vanity, because I had not, as yet, stopped to think whether I was pretty or not. It was the simple pleasure of my youthful self.

Birth Control

I cannot say why we didn't use birth control. We were both fully aware and knowledgeable. My parents and the community I lived in were always very open about sexual things, and I was never uneducated about *where babies come from*. I can only think that in our youthfulness and in our love, surrounded by the intoxicating beauty of the mountains and the lake, we simply never thought about it. I know I didn't.

Fifteen and Sixteen

I was fifteen when I became pregnant. He was sixteen. We were scared but we were happy. It seemed the most natural thing in the world to have a baby. We kept looking at my flat stomach, caressing it, kissing it, laughing, and thinking of the child we would have. We wanted the baby to be part of our wedding and so we planned to be married on May 1. Maybe we were young and naïve, but I do wonder what would have happened for us, and for the baby, if we had done as we had hoped.

Change

It was my mother who suggested it. She became firm and strong in a way I had never seen her before. She made the suggestion to change what, until that moment, I had no idea was changeable. She saw it as a choice between my life and the life of my child. I didn't know that a choice existed, and I was unclear as to why it had to be one or the other. No one asked me. It would not have mattered. I was too young. My voice was not strong like hers. I could not speak to oppose her.

Parenting

Perhaps our love would not have survived parenting a child, but then, neither of us survived *not* parenting one, either. The abortion hurled us into adulthood as if by initiation of the act itself. In the end, no one was saved—not myself, my young lover, or the baby. We were all destroyed.

The Tsunami Wave

After the abortion, and after my young lover left, I went inside of myself and stayed there for many years. I could no longer feel the clarifying angles and edges of myself. There seemed to be nothing about me to reveal to the world, or to etch myself out against the blue sky. Clarity left.

I tried not to let this happen to me, but it was like keeping a few feet ahead of a Tsunami wave. It did not matter that I refused to look back at the wave and acknowledge it there—poised, paused—for one blink of a second above my head. It did not matter because it was going to crash upon me with all its fury, whether I acknowledged it or not. Finally, I tipped my head and let it consume me completely. What else could I do? I was always a good swimmer, but one cannot swim in a Tsunami wave. All one can hope for is to survive.

Cleaning Fish

Some might blame my young lover for what happened. They might see him as cowardly and weak. They might say he should have been the one to speak. But he was like me—young and without a voice.

Since that time, I have known men who were truly cruel, truly mean. I have seen the difference between my young lover's gentle heart and their hard ones. These mean men reminded me of the fish I used to catch in the lake. When I cleaned a fish to eat it, I made one long cut down the stomach of the fish, and then I opened it up. When I did this, everything inside the fish fell out quickly in a pool of blood, as if none of the organs were attached, but just lying inside the fish's belly. That is what I think about some of the men I have known—one long cut along the center, from head to toe, and it would all fall out in a bloody, wadded-up heap.

But I knew if I were to cut my young lover open in the same way, out would spill emeralds, sapphires, rubies, and diamonds— each one cut to perfection—polished and gleaming, a treasure to behold and cherish.

The College

The college had a cafeteria that was a huge, round room, and every table had a vantage view of every other table. People stared at you as you ate your food. My roommate ate a salad every night with lettuce and tomato and gave me her purple onions. I taught her to put lemon juice on her salads instead of the Thousand Island dressing she was using and she fell in love with me. Or, so she said.

"Some of those mountain ways of yours come in handy, don't they?" she said to me, squeezing lemons on her lettuce. "Saves me loads of calories."

I did not tell her that it was not a mountain way.

I told her, as she was rolling her hair each morning, "I'll meet you for supper. I can help you with your biology then."

"You're so sweet," she said, winking at me in the mirror. "A little bizarre, but sweet. Come here, I'm gonna curl your hair."

She put her hands into my hair, lifted it up from the nape of my neck, and let it fall back down to my shoulders. It felt good. My grandmother used to braid my hair.

"This will keep the snakes out," she'd say, teasing me and smiling.

My hair hung wildly from my scalp, leaves and twigs stuck everywhere. My grandmother would brush for hours.

"That should do it," she would say, giving my back a pat to push me gently out from between her knees.

I could feel the braid swishing between my shoulder blades.

"Braid it for me," I said to my roommate.

"No way," she said, and smiled at me again in the mirror. "We're curling this. When I'm done, men will be crawling under our door."

Breakfast

Breakfast was good. The only people who rose early enough to eat it were the ones who probably did not eat lunch or supper for fear of the cafeteria's spotlight. It was a quiet time. All of us who were misplaced and frightened met in the cafeteria early each morning for breakfast. We did not speak or stare at one another as we ate. We were there for the anonymity and our growling stomachs.

We went to the back of the line, beyond where food was served for lunch and supper, into the recesses of the kitchen where the workers were. There, black women took our orders. I had eggs fried crispy around the edges, and pancakes with no syrup, just lots of butter. I liked my bacon real crunchy. The black women liked me.

They said, "Girl, you so skinny."

I stood waiting for my food, and watched them cooking and talking to one another. Their

bodies were large and soft, and I wanted to melt into their blackness. I wanted to tell them about my mornings at home. I wanted to tell them about the smell of the lake, and that sharp, sweet smell. I wanted to tell them about the feel of the mountain air holding you down under your quilts until morning would wait no longer and you had to rise. I wanted to tell them about my mother's soft, floured hands, and the biscuits we ate every day, along with the gentle splashing of the lake against the rocks. I wanted them to know the girl I used to be. I wanted them to see me, but these women didn't even know my name.

My roommate did not realize that I waited for her, starving, to eat supper.

She came into our dorm room and said, "I'm famished. Have you eaten yet?"

"No," I said, shrugging my shoulders and acting like it only just occurred to me that I had not eaten since breakfast.

She rolled her hair again before we left, and I felt as if I would faint before we got there. Sometimes she changed her clothes, putting on this or that, until she found the right thing.

She was never in a hurry for food. It was, as she put it, her "biggest battle."

I was scared and looking for the hands that had fed me all those years. I was cold from wanting to be back in my mother's kitchen and to smell the sweet hot tea on her breath. I was a scavenger looking for food, but unlike the buzzard's wise and deliberate search—circling high and slow with a patience and confidence terrifying to its dying prey below—I was aimless in my wanderings.

Looking For A Husband

My roommate was looking for a husband. She wasn't the prettiest girl at the college but she *was* confident she would get her guy. I was confident, too. She was the color of fall—all gold and gleaming browns like the forest floor freshly covered with autumn's new leaves. She had a big toothy smile, long thick brown hair the color of dark caramel, and a very curvy body. She had quite a few advantages that the other girls didn't have—determination actually being foremost—even over the curvy body.

Another Young Lover?

I was not looking for a husband. I was searching for myself, and so I began to search in the last place I remembered being—in love and happy. I suppose I thought that another young lover would help me, or that another young lover would see me hiding deep inside and coax me out. This did not happen.

I did not find another young lover. Instead, I found silly boys who were spoiled—because they had been told untrue things about themselves. They had been taught that success lay with the world and their achievements. They had been taught to be selfish and they had plans. They were going to be doctors, lawyers, businessmen, and clergy. Nothing would interfere with their futures. The color of their lovemaking was like the dirty water that washes down the road after a storm—dingy brown.

I slept with these boys.

Breaking Hearts

I learned that boredom meant good-bye, and that saying good-bye was no more than ignoring you after a night of lovemaking. So I broke hearts before they could break mine. I kept them entertained until I grew bored, and then I exchanged that boy for another one.

Two Hundred and Fifty Dollars

Alcohol would have been cheaper. A quart of liquor costs ten, or maybe twenty bucks if you had it on you, an abortion, two hundred and fifty dollars, always the same price. I wondered why the price stayed the same. Why didn't it ever get any cheaper, like calculators, or more expensive, like cars? I quit bothering to ask when I called the clinic. I just made the appointment.

My Future

The world said this was the best choice, because of my age and my potential future. But when I looked in the mirror, I wondered, what future? I questioned whose choice this really was? Was it my parents', or the boys', or mine? As yet, no one has asked me.

Art History

I fell in love again. Here was the young lover I had been hoping for. Here was the one who could bring me out of my darkness. There was color again. There was the reverence and play of light—a thought, a feeling, a pause, a turn of the head, an emotion captured, timeless, and reaching beyond the centuries to open a soul and bring a young girl out. My heart pounded and I knew I had seen that same light streaming through the green leaves of the trees, hesitating on a windowsill, and changing the colors of the lake. I had seen that same look in my young lover's eyes—that same sunlight flirting around his face, and reflecting the line of his cheekbone and the curve of his jaw.

This was my Art History class.

The Hateful Professor

There was one moment when I felt myself awaken—almost with a start—at the college. I heard my voice and saw myself again. It was in an Art History class.

On the first day, the professor said, "If you are a freshman, please leave. You will fail my class. Your counselors will help you find another one."

One freshman did not take his words seriously, or else he considered himself above such, and the professor actually picked up the student's books, handed them to him, and then ushered him out.

He said, "If you are a sophomore, your IQ had better be higher than mine if you want to stay in this class and not fail."

No one dared ask just how high his IQ was, and another round of students departed. I was a junior. He had not gotten to me yet, and I was curious what he would have to say.

He said, "If you are a junior or a senior, you damn well better stay, and you damn well better plan on working your ass off if you want to pass this class."

This meant nothing to me. I had stopped caring a long time ago about whether I passed or not. My straight A's from high school were now C's and D's. I could bide my time in his classroom as easily as I could anywhere else.

The hateful professor started with slides—thousands of slides of paintings, buildings, and sculptures. He said we would be tested on all of them, and he required us to tell the period, the style, the artist, the school, the influence, the origin, and the medium—absolutely any and all details. Each day, he gleefully darkened the room and clicked on his slide projector. The world of art would flash before our eyes. We furiously took notes and marked the various slides in our books.

Each day as I stepped into his classroom, I felt myself becoming alive again. I was breathing the air of my mountains. I was swimming in deep water. I heard my voice ask questions, and I saw myself study slides outside the art rooms.

I watched the art students silently work on their paintings and sculptures. I yearned for their world, with its high windows and clutter. I sat for hours outside those rooms studying slides, while they sat inside, working diligently.

I got up my nerve and went to see the hateful professor. It seemed to me that my whole life hung on my question and I was sick to my stomach.

I asked, "Is it possible to get an Art History degree?"

He did not raise his head at my question, but continued looking at the papers on his desk. Then, he said, "What medium do you work in?"

"Huh? Oh. I don't know. I mean, I don't have one. See, I'm not actually an artist. I mean, I've never painted or sculpted, or well, anything, really. But I really, really love the Art History class and thought maybe I could get a degree in that."

"You thought wrong," he said. "You must be an artist who is majoring in Art, and then possibly have a minor in Art History."

He continued reading, and I knew I was dismissed. I said nothing else. The small spark that his class had awakened in me was gone, and again, myself with it.

Chosen

Suddenly, I wanted to know why this was so important to her.

"Brenda," I said.

"Hmmm?" she answered.

"Why are you looking for a husband?"

"Oh," she said, as if I had caught her at something and she wasn't quite sure whether to lie her way out or simply tell the truth.

Since I had never seen her lie, she settled on the truth.

"You'll think I'm silly," she said, hesitating for a second but then deciding to try me out. "It's because I've always wanted to be chosen."

"Chosen?"

"Yeah, you know, somebody actually picks you out of a crowd and thinks to themselves, 'Now there is someone I want to spend the rest of my life with.' Remember how in grammar school you used to stand there, waiting to be chosen for someone's team, just dying inside, hoping that somebody would notice you? I guess it's like that in a way. The way I figure it is, as women, we only have a short period of time for some guy to notice us and then what? If I wait like some of these girls are talking about, until I've established a career and all that, well, I'll be in my thirties. Now you tell me. Which would a guy choose—someone young, fresh and pretty, or some woman exhausted from trying to keep up and make her mark in a world that just happened to be a man's world anyway?"

She was quiet for a moment, deciding, I guessed, whether to expose her deepest thoughts or not.

Then she plunged ahead and said, "Ivy, have you ever wanted a man to get down on his knees with the most beautiful ring in the world, picked out just for you, and ask you to spend the rest of your life with him because there was no one else he would rather spend the rest of his life with?"

She looked so pretty right then. Her make-up, hair, shoes, and everything matched. She was going out on a date and she had made herself beautiful. I wondered if he would notice how pretty she really was—I mean pretty on the inside—or if he would only appreciate how good she made him look.

"Yeah," I said. "Yeah, I would like that."

Loose Girls

My parents sat in the crowd. My father was waving madly as I walked down the aisle to receive my college diploma. My mother sat distant, and still unforgiving. I thought maybe she had known all along, even before the abortion. Maybe she had already thought to herself that I was just another loose girl. As for me, I was just finding out.

Following Road Maps

I dated a boy once who was highly successful and I was entranced with his ability to achieve whatever he put his mind to. He failed at nothing. I asked him how he did this, and how it was that he thrived in a world where others barely choked their way through another day.

He replied, "I think some people are born with a road map in their heads. I know I was. I have always known where I was going and how to get there."

"And so you just followed this inborn map of yours and it got you where you were going?" I asked.

"Yeah, I guess so, but it wasn't as easy as it sounds. You do have to stop sometimes and study the map, try to read it right, and then make choices. You can't avoid making choices, Ivy, or I guess you can, but then you would go nowhere. You would end up standing in the same place all the time, and letting things happen to you, instead of making things happen. Choices determine where we're going in life. They're what move us along. You know, Ivy, not everyone is watching the world fly by their window. Some people are actually driving the car."

He meant me, though he may not have realized it, but I had made a choice—one I couldn't live with. I really didn't think I could ever risk another one. Besides, I had never been good at reading maps. Even when I tried to read one, I always searched for water and traced its route, wondering what body of water it longed to.

The Islands

The islands were soft pink, piercing blue, with frightening swirls of gray and black, pure white, coral and bottomless holes of green. There were fish of every color you could think of—red, blue, yellow, and purple. When you killed them, their color drained out and they looked like any other fish—like the basses and small brim I caught in the lake.

I did not swim in the blue water with the white bottom.

Daniel said, "You can't swim, and you grew up with a lake in your front yard. I'd be ashamed."

I did not tell him I couldn't swim. He thought that himself.

Daniel

It was easy to fall in love with Daniel because he was happy. Other than my college roommate, he was the only other person I knew who was. Life seemed to roll off him like the gentle waves of the ocean where he was from. Daniel had a lot of friends, a lot of money, a finger that had been cut off in an accident, and a wife. I ignored the wife part as long as I could, which turned out to be about two years in all.

He picked me up from school in his Mercedes 450SL convertible, always with the top down.

He'd say, "Come on, I'll carry you to eat."

He said "carry" where other people said "drive."

Daniel made sure I was fed. He said I was the only person he knew who could eat one meal while planning the next one. He took good care of me.

You and Me, Girl

I tried to act like a car that cost more than my house was a perfectly normal thing, but it was hard not to want to touch its silkiness. It was hard not to ask point-blank how much something like that cost.

"Let's get out of here, so we can talk," he said.

"Talk about what?" I asked.

"Us," he said. "You and me, girl, that's what."

Then he leaned over and kissed me. He kissed me as if he wanted to—as if he had wanted to do that for a long time. I liked it when he said "us."

Pick a Pretty Girl

"Well, you see," I told Daniel, "I'm tired."

I already liked Daniel and I didn't want him to think he was getting something he wasn't. I wanted to be honest with him.

"I mean really tired, like deep down tired. I've done a lot of bad things and when you do bad things for a long time, well, after a while it makes you weary inside. Like you lost something very important—your life or maybe yourself, I don't know. It makes you tired and sometimes it's hard to see a thing clearly, you know, to really know what it is you want. All I want is not to hurt and maybe sleep peacefully for a change. I know a lot of people think of me as a party girl, but really, I'm not. I just pretend. See, sometimes I don't want to get up and sometimes I don't even want to live. Maybe you should pick another girl to live with you on your boat—one who isn't tired—a pretty blonde girl who is happy and carefree and could be your party girl."

Daniel pushed my bangs out of my eyes (a habit I would remember fondly) and said,

"Come on, girl. Let me carry you home. Then tomorrow we'll leave for the islands, okay? You'll love the islands, I promise."

A Good Day

Daniel kept his boat at George's Marina, an unusual name for a marina in the middle of the Caribbean, I thought. Nobody could ever remember seeing George. A guy named Paul with a gold "P" on his front tooth ran the place. The locals liked to speculate quite a bit about George.

Some believed he was dead and that now the marina belonged to no one, which unofficially meant it belonged to Paul. Others said George owned a car lot in Ohio that covered sixty acres and he was too busy to check on the marina. He couldn't possibly leave Ohio with that many cars to look after.

"Sixty acres, man," they said, "is a lot of cars. He's too busy to come here and fix up the place, and make it nice like the new marinas. Still, he misses the islands, hey? He misses the islands."

Fishing was Daniel's truest love, and Paul was known to be the best fisherman in the islands. We fished all day for the marlins and tunas. Sometimes we spent the whole day chasing just one fish. Daniel sat strapped in the swiveling chair at the back of the boat and Paul was up top driving and watching. I generally sat on the ladder that led up to where Paul was, between the two of them.

Paul would shout, "Daniel, my man, you got to wait for that zing! Listen for that zing before you pull. When you hear that, then you know he took the bait. Then the fight is on, and then we'll see who the real man is."

At night, after a good day of fishing, we would sit on the top deck, with our chairs pulled together. We draped our legs over one another's, while watching a perfect ball-shaped sun drop into the ocean. (We never missed a sunrise, either.) With our chairs facing east this time, and sipping coffee, we watched that same ball slip back into place in the uncluttered horizon of the blue sky.

Daniel would sip his gin and grapefruit, and say, "You got to listen for that zing!"

I knew that meant it had been a good day for him.

Supper

Supper did not officially start until the sun had gone down. Then, Daniel, with his usual passion for everything, got things started. He put me in charge of cutting up vegetables, shelling shrimp, opening oysters and clams and cleaning the fish—which he hated to do, but which I had done my whole life. It was no worse to me than making patties out of raw hamburger meat.

Daniel said, "I like a woman who can clean a fish!"

Meanwhile, he heated the cooking oil to a crackle, and started making sauces. He dug around for this pot, then that one, decided on rice or potatoes (generally rice) and talked the whole time. Food decisions, because he loved to cook, were hard for Daniel and he would go back and forth for quite awhile between a white sauce or a little lemon and dill. Starting the grill or not could be a whole conversation in itself, filled with the nuances of, "Do we want to mess with that? I probably should have started it earlier. Nah, it will make dinner late and we'll be starving. I'll just fry it in cornmeal." And then, "Oh hell, what's the hurry? I'll start the grill. Good with you, girl? Do you mind waiting?"

I shook my head no. I never minded waiting. I was happy waiting. It was my favorite time of the day. I was generally perched on a bar stool, my legs pulled up to my chest with my sweatshirt pulled down over my knees, and my chin resting on them. I loved the smell of his cooking, the fish frying, the vegetables sautéing silently, and his whisking of the sauces. I loved to listen to him then, not his words so much as the sound of his voice in the dimming of the day.

Not My Choice

Daniel seemed to know that I had lost my way. He told me I was an angel who had flown too close to the ground (that was a song he liked) and after I was better—after I didn't hurt so much anymore—I would leave him. That was not true. He was not mine to leave or not to leave; he loved his wife—the 'woman', he called her, and he belonged to her. She was the one who had the choice to leave or stay, not me.

Real

He kept his wife very separate from his life with me. He never mentioned her name, never called her when I was around, never ignored me to be with her, and never told me where they lived. I only knew she was real because I looked in his wallet once and saw a picture of her. She was beautiful—very tall, like him, with dark hair and big brown eyes. The picture was of the two of them and he had his arm around her neck pulling her to him and laughing in the same way he did with me.

Daniel's Language

He would coax me into imitating the boys at school. He loved to hear me make fun of them.

So I would lower my voice and say, "After I graduate from here—at the top of my class, of course—I'm headed to law school then an MBA. Then when I'm with the best firm, making six figures, I figure I'll settle down, have the wife and the two point one kids, but for right now why don't you come on over here and satisfy yourself with the big guy? He's just waiting on you to let him do his job."

Daniel would roar with laughter and ask, "And how big was the big guy?"

"Don't ask," I'd say laughing, "it's too sad for words."

"There had to be one guy who wasn't so full of shit."

"There was actually. I remember when I told him no, he didn't push or start all that, oh-come-on-you-know-you-want-to business.' He just said, 'Okay,' and then asked me if I wanted to go get a hamburger."

"Did you?"

"Yeah, we went to Krystal Burgers and ate those square hamburgers that only cost a quarter a piece. He couldn't believe how many I ate."

"Poor guy probably used every quarter he had to feed you."

Daniel loved to watch me eat.

"What happened to him?"

"He transferred, I think. I don't know, can't remember."

"Well, for my sake, I'm glad. But he sounds like a keeper."

I stayed in the islands for two years and then it was time to go. Daniel cried when I left. I had never seen him cry before. Tears fell down his cheeks from behind his Ray-Ban sunglasses and I was surprised and pleased to see how much I had meant to him.

He said, "I love us."

"Me, too," I said.

Daniel's language was laughter and even now, many years later, I can close my eyes and hear his laugh and see his smile.

I left the islands and returned home. It was time to start my future.

Professionalism

Each day I put on my suit of professionalism and opened the doors of my employment. I had only to appear like there was no other place on earth I'd rather be and that no other person's needs interested me more than the clients we were serving. I did this easily as it was only more pretense, and pretense was my language.

Still, I was trying to find a way, some way to live. So I started to work out, to ride my bicycle up mountains, to run, and to lift weights. I ran marathons, did triathlons, and ate only a little rice and vegetables.

Connection

With the boys in college, I had tried to connect emotionally to find the girl who had looked into her young lover's eyes, and now I tried to connect physically with her. I tried to find the body of the girl who had felt her thighs sting as she climbed the mountains of Alarka Laurel, and who had felt her lungs pushed to bursting as she swam deeper and deeper in Alarka Laurel Lake.

I wanted to inhabit her body again. She had been solid, unencumbered, and physical. Since so many unkind hands had been on my body and so many babies sucked out of it, that my body was marked, imprints had been left behind. I wasn't trying to be a supermodel. I was trying to salvage and reclaim.

Anorexia

It was hard for the doctors and my parents to understand that I did not have anorexia. It was hard for them to understand that I did not want to die. I simply wanted to live. I did not want to look like the world told me to look. I wanted to look like myself. I spent countless hours in counselors' offices talking about the proper image of myself and how those women in the magazines, "don't even look like that."

I finally quit talking and just shook my head yes, yes. This satisfied them and they felt successful that finally one girl, at least, had understood that she could look however she chose. She didn't have to copy models or actresses. When they discharged me, they admonished me to avoid all "those magazines." They had no idea that I had never even looked at one.

Sex

He said, "Do you like sex?"

He was old enough to be my grandfather and so coked up that he had to hold onto the boat's railing to steady himself. I half expected his eyeballs to start rolling around in his head, like the girl in *The Exorcist*. He was trying so hard to see clearly that he was squinting.

I didn't answer because no one had ever asked me that question before, and although I knew it wasn't what he meant—he had wanted to know if I would have sex with him, but the drugs had him confused. The abruptness of his question made me wonder, did I? I discovered in that moment that I did not.

I understood then that sex had become as all the other things in my life—pretense. The lovemaking of my youth had been replaced with strangers groping in the dark and sneaking out before dawn. I could see no real reason to continue with such pretense, so I replied, "No, not really."

He managed to pull his wallet out, an astonishing feat actually, in his condition, and handed me a thousand dollars.

"Do you like it now?" he asked.

The Angry Man

People, especially women, loved this man. They loved his money and his good looks. He was tall and thin, like a grassy reed swaying by the water. But when he took his clothes off, he was very solid and big. He made me forget my image which had been a nice one.

He never lied to me. I knew from the beginning that he slept with other women—lots of them—and not just me. I lived in his house, but he was in their beds as much as he was in ours. I did not care about the other women. I was with him because I could no longer even pretend at my life, and he filled in all the gaps. He never asked anything from me except that I show up when he needed me. He wanted me to look pretty. That seemed easy enough and so I did. Between his money and his ability to control his world, I was not bothered with even the most mundane things.

He was the angry man. His language was anger. His job required that he make very hard decisions every day and he was very good at it. He liked to make decisions and he never allowed anyone to choose—even in something as trivial as where to eat dinner. He was happiest this way. So I let him take over. I let him choose everything. I understood his desire to control his world. I would have liked to control my own.

I liked the authority he had with other people and his job, and the check he kept on his emotions. It made me feel safe and protected me from the insanity of my own world.

I did not ask him for anything and that seemed to please him. He seemed to admire me for that, as if I had too much pride to ask anybody for anything. He thought that was a good thing. He didn't understand that I simply wouldn't have known what to ask for.

Waiting Patiently

The angry man's swimming pool was perfectly blue with pink and white flowers encircling it. I sat for hours undisturbed, and surrounded by the flawlessness of wealth. I watched the water ripple imperceptibly from a slight breeze, but I did not swim in the enticingly clear and still water.

The housekeeper said, "You waiting patient."

She thought I sat this way waiting on the angry man who always came home late from work. She did not know that I was dead and not waiting on anything.

Jealousy

Women were always coming on to him. They gave him their phone numbers, saying to ditch me and give them a call.

He always thought this was funny and once he said to me, "One of the reasons I like you is that you don't ever get jealous. If you were another woman—like some of the women I've dated— we'd be in a fight by now."

We were headed home from a wedding reception when he said this. I was driving because he was drunk. At the reception, a woman had offered him oral sex—if only he would get rid of me for the evening. I hadn't said a word. I just stood there holding the car keys, and waited to see if he was coming home with me or going with her. I remember looking at the azalea bushes in bloom, and made a mental note to ask John, his gardener, about the unusual lavender-colored one. I had not seen that color before.

He finally decided to come with me and this is when he told me he liked me because I never got jealous. I looked at him, surprised that he didn't know, though I should have known he thought all women were in love with him.

But I said, "It's because I'm not in love with you. If I loved you, I'd be jealous and sad, the same as anybody."

This made him very angry. He never loved women or had fond feelings for them. He expected them to love him and so he got very angry which he was prone to do when he was drunk anyway. I knew that when we got home, he would "teach me a lesson."

Falling In Love?

He was still thinking about what I had said in the car.

"You just said that because you really *are* jealous and that is your way of getting back at me, isn't it?" he said winking and grinning, like he had caught me at trying to play coy.

This was after he had forced me to have sex with him, without my diaphragm—even though I told him I needed it. That was how he took his anger out on me, by forcing me to have sex with him. We were sitting in his living room with a fire going. I was lying on his wrap-around couch, covered up with a blanket. My feet were pointed at the fire, and I was drinking hot chocolate. To some, it may have looked like the picture of domestic bliss.

"Said what?"

"That you don't love me, but if you did, you would have been jealous—the same as any other woman."

"*You* don't love *me*," I said, bringing up something personal for the first time in our relationship and wondering what his response would be.

"I never fall in love with anyone."

"Then why care if I love you or not?"

"Because it's different for women."

"What's different?"

"Women fall in love if you look at them."

"Men don't fall in love?"

"Some pathetic losers do, but no decent woman would want one of those. See, women like to be dominated. They like to be bossed around. Oh, they pretend that they don't, but get one in bed and then she talks a different story. She wants you to be in control."

He talked this way a lot and mostly I just ignored it. I thought he had no more idea what women wanted than any other man I had ever met. He just had way more confidence about the whole thing.

"What does control have to do with falling in love?" I asked.

"Well, if you go and fall in love, then you mess up the whole system. Then it becomes more about trying to please and less about being the boss."

"Would trying to please be so bad?"

"It would if it meant having to fall in love. Think about it. I try to please you all the time. I think about pleasing you everyday, but my emotions aren't all caught up in it."

This was true. He saw to it that I lacked for nothing. He remembered the movies and books I liked, and the food I wanted. He had even made me the hot chocolate.

"Have you ever been in love?" I asked.

"No."

"What about Susannah, your college girlfriend. I thought you loved her."

"I probably thought so, too, but I was only nineteen at the time. I imagine it was more lust than love. She did, after all, have that body."

"So what will you say about me when I'm gone?"

"Are you going somewhere?"

He was looking at me over his glass of wine. He never drank things like hot chocolate. He drank wine or gin and tonic. I could tell I had touched a nerve. Women didn't leave him.

"I don't suppose we'll be together forever," I said. "It hardly seems your style. I imagine you'll find another one soon enough; one you will like better than me; one out of your current crop."

It was the first time I had ever mentioned his other women.

He ignored my comment but answered my question.

"I'd say I like you. I just like you, Ivy. I like having you around."

He should have stopped there. I might have actually stayed, but he went on.

"You don't bug me like all the others."

Then he patted like my leg, as if to reassure me. I wondered about what.

He meant that I never asked him for anything—nothing—not love, not tenderness, not caring and, most especially, not money. He called the women he thought were after his money "gold diggers". He liked the fact that I wasn't a "gold digger."

Exactly two months after the angry man had made me have sex with him, I discovered I was pregnant. It seemed I had become pregnant despite his assurance that I would not. He said to abort the baby.

"My career is at a crucial point," he said. "A baby would break me right now."

I looked at this tall angry man who spoke the language of power, sitting on his enormous leather couch, and looking worried for once.

I said, "All it takes is a baby to break your world?"

I left. I could not abort another child. My voice saved this one. I believed at the time that I was saving my baby's life. I realized later that I had saved both the baby's…and mine.

He said good-bye, and though he did not speak it, again I felt he was grateful that I had asked him for nothing. Neither this baby, nor myself, would interfere. So he watched me walk away. His money meant so much to him. It was his first and only love. That was okay because I did not love money, and so I suppose it would have never worked anyway.

Waking Up

I understood better, after having my child, why my mother had insisted on an abortion. You have a baby and nothing belongs to you anymore—not your body, your mind, or your time. It does not matter if you are tired, sad, or on a pilgrimage to find your lost self. The baby needs food, potty training, help with homework, a map of the world, and thousands of questions answered. There is no part of yourself that you can hold back. You must give everything.

With the rest of the world, I could stand there talking, and look interested. I could say interesting things, and the entire time I was asleep. I could not do that with a baby. A baby will scream until you wake with a start, out of your sleep, out of your numbness, and say to yourself, "What? What is it?" You cannot shut down when you have a baby. You must come alive. And so, with a baby, I did. I came alive. I began to wake up.

Madonna

The first thing I did when I started waking up was to buy a house. It was not an expensive house, but it was a nice one, painted blue on the outside and yellow on the inside. It felt good to us—my child and myself.

It had a wonderful porch. It was long, flat and wide. It followed the full front of the house and along one side, which led to a small garden. My child learned to walk and then run on this porch, on little fat legs, up and down the long verandah. There were a lot of windows in our house and I hung prisms across the curtain rods instead of drapes. My child loved for me to spin the prisms and play "Catch a Rainbow."

I suddenly felt like every picture of every Madonna ever painted.

The second thing I did was to teach myself to cook. I started with bread. It seemed a good place to start and it was. Children love bread because it is filling and rich—very earthy and satisfying to the soul. I loved to make it because I could stand at the kitchen counter, kneading the dough, sprinkling flour across the sticky substance and kneading again, feeling as though I was finally providing for a life. I was nourishing a life into being, instead of destroying one. I was cooking, I suppose, for all my children, born and unborn.

Finally, I made a garden. I remembered the angry man's gardener and I did as he did. I created in our garden the picture I had in my head. I made a huge number of mistakes, learning, for instance, that the frangipani and bougainvillea I had loved in the islands do not live through a winter in the mountains. Still, it turned out very nice and my child liked the garden best of all.

I took the pebbles and shells I had brought back from the islands and encircled the beds. I made small paradises of pansies, sweet peas, and hollyhocks—a gift from the rich man.

Gardeners

I found the world of gardeners in books, in my neighbors down the road, and at local nurseries.

I had never met anyone who planted a garden like Monet had painted a picture, with deliberation and execution, except John, the angry man's gardener. I was left with the impression that only rich people had gardens for pleasure.

My neighbors planted their own gardens. The people who worked at the nurseries did, too. They were artists. Their gardens were their medium and they worked as diligently at their craft as the artists who sat in their rooms with the high windows and clutter. So, at last, I had found my medium, and I wondered what the hateful professor would say about that.

Quiet Times

There were many hours spent quietly between myself and my child—my child gesturing excitedly with little hands, stomping in the creek, playing in the forts, and sitting in trees—myself in the kitchen or garden. These were peaceful, comforting hours, and I stopped many times to say, "Thank you." I said thank you to the angry man, the rich man, to the world, to God, and to whomever you thanked for such a gift as a child and a blue house with yellow walls.

Saying Good-bye

There were still men in my life, though honestly, I don't know why. My child completely filled my world and I was happy now, as I had not been in a long time. These men never met my child, and I never told my child about them.

I remember how easy it was to go from saying, "I love you," to barely "Good-bye." The good-bye's became for me a waiting process. I had been silent for so long and I had not spoken the truth in so long, that I did not know how to simply say, "Leave." Instead, I pretended to care, when I rarely gave him a thought in my day. When I wanted a man to be gone, I would wait for him to say good-bye and eventually he always did.

I had first silenced myself for my parents, and for their ideas of what my future would look like. I found that I remained silent for the men in my life.

Seven Men in All

There were seven men in all—I mean of the ones I remember distinctively. The others I remember only vaguely, or not at all.

When I was with these men, it was necessary that I pretend. Or, I felt it was necessary, anyway. I feared they would leave if I did not. It was like playing a part. When I got tired of playing the part, our relationship would dissolve—until number seven.

Number seven came and he did not leave. I made the usual excuses about my child and he smiled but did not go away. He said he would like to meet my child someday.

I thought, well then, he has other women and that is why he is in no hurry to leave. So I began to call him at odd hours and he always answered the phone. He was happy to sit and talk for awhile. Once I called and he was making flower boxes for his front windows. I could hear his drill in the background. He was painting them green to match the trim on his house, he had said.

I began to call more often after that, and generally he was making something with wood because he liked the smell and the feel of wood, and because that is what he did. He made furniture. I showed him how to rub his hand across a flower and then smell his fingers. This pleased him immensely because he could smell and touch at the same time.

I kept waiting and waiting for him to say good-bye. I waited for his patience with a child not his own to end, for his desire to make flower boxes to turn into a desire for other women, money, or far-away lands. But always his words stayed the same. He was always in the garage making something with wood.

My child did meet this man and liked him very much, and so did I.

My child said, "Mommy, he is a sweet man."

And he is. He is my sweet man.

Sometimes I became frightened that he would say good-bye. When I felt like that, he would give me a big hug. I was all wrapped up inside his arms where I could smell wood chips and flannel.

He said, "Ah, I'm not going anywhere."

He didn't, either. He moved into our blue house with my child, and he built a workshop near the garden—for inspiration, he said. He liked having us near while he worked. He filled our blue house with the smell of wood and stain. It was a happy smell.

My sweet man's language was love. Love poured out like the water I poured on my garden. I was careful to pour it in such a way that the roots of my flowers would get watered, and not just the blooms. I could not help but feel myself loved, expanding, reaching out, breathing deep, and making room to take it all in. His love reached places that seemed impossible to heal.

The Women

Each day when I got home from work, my sweet man met me on the front porch with a glass of iced tea and said, "Well, what did *the women* do today?"

He meant this nicely. He was happy that I had made new friends—something I had not done in a long time—had friends. He called them, "Love and Reason."

He said, "So how are Love and Reason?" as he handed me a glass of iced tea and settled into a porch chair to hear about my day.

I told my sweet man, "They don't have any holes; no empty spaces. I don't mean they're happy, and that their lives are perfect. After all, Love is going through a divorce and Reason wants to be pregnant, but can't. I just mean, well, they're not empty. I don't think they got lost like I did."

"Maybe they hide it better than most people."

"I never see any holes in their eyes."

"Huh," my sweet man said quietly, understanding what I meant.

I had seen sadness, confusion, and hurt, in my friends' eyes, but never did I even have a glimpse of the black holes that stretched on in my own soul, like the black holes in space— empty, bottomless, and horrifying. They had suffered, and were suffering, I suppose. No one was immune to that; yet they had themselves. I began to realize that not everyone had lost themselves along the way.

Hiding

Sometimes, alone in my garden or in my blue house napping, I thought I heard footsteps. I would go to investigate because I knew I was the only one home at the time, but no one was ever there. This happened so frequently that I told my sweet man about it. I told him that I heard footsteps behind me when I was at the kitchen sink. I had seen a shadow crossing the floor as I came out of the bedroom. But I could find no evidence of anyone being there, and there was no reason for worry.

My sweet man said, "Perhaps it is the fifteen-year-old girl that you lost, who is peeping out from behind you to see if it is safe now."

Circle of Love

I watched them spinning in the grass. The daylight was fading fast, and darkness descended. Yet, for once, I was not afraid of the dark sky forming above my house. My child held onto his arms as they spun.

My child screamed with delight, "Faster, Faster!"

They were beautiful, the two of them. They were my life, and it seemed to me as if they were making a glorious circle of love.

Only Blue

After developing the black-and-white photographs, the photographer took one picture that he particularly liked. He tinted the overalls of my child, and then my eyes, blue. He left the rest of the picture alone, so that blue was the only color. It was beautiful and I offered to buy it from him, understanding that this was his artistry. Yet, he refused and gave it to me as a gift. He had put it in a pretty wooden frame.

I hung the picture in our hallway and studied it every time I passed. It seemed the black-and-white photograph I had so often thought of as my life, had colors creeping into it, and I wondered, after all these many years, what these colors might be.

Christians

She said something interesting. She was always so confident and so sure that I could never imagine her losing herself to the world around her. I thought maybe it was because of her faith, and because she was a Christian. So I mentioned this to her. I asked her if this was the reason she had never lost herself, because she was a Christian; because she believed in Jesus, and somehow that protected her in a world where people lost themselves every day.

She said, "Oh, no, I don't think so. Christians aren't any more immune to losing themselves than anyone else is. If we do get lost, we at least have someone to come find us."

"Who?" I asked, curious to know who would do such a thing.

"Jesus," she said.

Jesus

I found something else in the world, too—Jesus. He had slipped into my heart without my even noticing, until one day in June when I suddenly realized I was talking to him while pulling weeds in my garden. It startled me. I hadn't known he was there. I could sense him laughing, as if he thought my surprise was funny, and it delighted him. I told him if he was going to show up unexpected like that, then he could at least help pull weeds. This made him laugh again.

When Jesus laughs, it is like swimming across the lake while a soft summer rain drizzles down over your face.

A Voiceless Cry

"Why do you think he came?" my sweet man asked.

"Who? Jesus?" I asked.

"Yeah," he said, tilting his head in curiosity.

"Oh," I said. "I hadn't thought about why, really." It had seemed to me that he had always been there, and I just hadn't known it until he showed himself to me.

"Well, maybe he heard my cry," I said.

"You mean you prayed?"

"No, I didn't pray," I said, searching for the right words. "It was more like a voiceless cry."

"A voiceless cry?" he asked.

"Yeah," I said, figuring it out as I went. "That makes sense, doesn't it?"

"I don't know. Does it?"

"Well, who else but Jesus would find the person who can't even cry out? Only he would hear the voiceless cry, I think."

"Yeah, that makes sense. I like that," my sweet man said, smiling at me.

"Yeah," I said, smiling back. "I like that, too."

Language

My language, for most of my life, had been pretense. Now, in order to get better, the therapist with three names said I would need the language of honesty. I was afraid of honesty. I was afraid of the pain that lay underneath all that pretense.

To get well, I could no longer pretend that babies had not been sucked out of my body. I could not be indifferent to the pain of offering my body to men who had only used it. I could not conveniently forget that I had drunk alcohol and done drugs—all in an attempt to forget. I had ripped layer after layer off myself—each one made up of lies I had told myself were necessary for my survival at the time. However, they were destroying me now. It was time to speak for myself, but I didn't know how to bring the words out that had been lodged inside of me for so long.

So I made pictures.

Rape

I was raped once, not by one man, but by three. After this happened, I went to a counselor. I went because I wanted to sit quietly with someone. I wanted to sit quietly until the horror in my mind became a murmur and not a scream. I wanted to sit quietly until my breathing returned. I wanted to sit quietly and reintroduce calm. I wanted to be able to hear birds sing outside my window again and not jump at the sound.

I told this woman—the counselor—what had happened to me. I suppose I was hoping that she would take my hand and sit with me. She didn't. Instead, she pointed to some big pillows in her office that were on the floor by her couch. She said she kept those pillows for situations like mine and that I could punch the pillows until I was no longer angry about being raped.

"But I'm not angry," I said.

She replied, "I would be very angry if that had happened to me. It's okay to be angry. Try not to be afraid of your anger."

She didn't know what she was saying. She didn't understand. Many years later, after this has happened to me, I am still not angry. I am terrified.

I am terrified of being dropped straight down into hell. I am terrified of complete blackness and complete separation. I am terrified of the pain that one man, or three, had caused. I am terrified of being devoured, and that my screams were silenced.

I am terrified of hands reaching out to harm me, of appetites so voracious they stop at nothing to feed themselves—not even the sounds of ripping flesh, like hyenas. I am terrified of fists pounding into my head again and again, of being slammed against a wall. I am terrified of the penis of some faceless man being crammed into my mouth while I silently beg God, the world, and somebody, to either let me go or let me die. I am terrified at how the value of my life could change in an instant. I am terrified at how insignificant my life is in the hands of an enemy, or worse, in the hands of indifference.

No amount of anger therapy will work when one has seen the jaws of hell. One does not stomp one's foot and yell injustice. One turns and runs, never hesitating, and never looking back, but running to save your life.

Giving It to Jesus

This is what I did with my rape—I gave it to Jesus. I said, "Here, you take it," and I walked away. There was really no other way.

When my child is worried about something that is too big for a child to worry over, I say, "That is a Mommy worry. You give that worry to me."

My child will ask in return, "So what are my worries?"

I think about this for a minute, studying the ceiling and tapping my foot as if trying to think of something, and then I might say, "Well, you have to worry if your mother will make spinach quiche for supper, and if your room is clean."

"Oh, Mom," my child responds, "you never make spinach quiche, and you never clean your room, either."

Being raped is a Jesus worry. It is too big for me. If I feel it starting to creep back into my thinking, and if I feel it trying to crawl inside my mind again and take from me all the things my life is becoming, I stop and say a prayer. I give it to Jesus again.

Anxiety Attacks

They came suddenly and unexpected. The doctors called them anxiety attacks. To me, they were earthquakes inside my body, re-shifting and reshaping the landscape. I felt most days as if I stood on my head looking at the world upside down.

I held onto the bed in a dizzying attempt to stop the spinning, and to control the earthquakes, but they kept coming—one after the other. Daytime and nighttime they came. It didn't matter—time meant nothing to them. Whether it was schedules or responsibilities, they rendered you incapable of even the smallest task. It was impossible to explain why, why you simply couldn't go on.

Mostly, though, they came in the calmest part of the evening—when supper was just finishing and the world was turning the dusty color of purple. People were beginning to still their minds. I would sit in the garden then, behind the blooming foxgloves, trying to breathe, while waiting for each earthquake to pass, and to settle itself. I hated them, but I think they were a sign—a sign that the old was leaving and the new was moving in.

The Veil

We stared at the pictures, and at the startling beauty of them. It seemed to us as if the artist had peeled back the veil that God had placed between himself and his creation to reveal what paradise had looked like before the fall. The paintings were raw and simple. The colors were deep and piercing. Their images were haunting. All of that was inside of me, I thought. I had never known.

The therapist with the three names smiled as she said, "All that."

"Yeah," I said, "all that."

Mothers

There were several pictures of mothers with their children—happy, silly, carefree, arms giving hugs, smiles, noses pressed against noses, clapping baby's hands, splashing in the water, running down the beach, twirling round and round, and so many things a mother could do with her children. She smiled at these pictures.

"Happy pictures," she said.

"Yes," I said, staring out her window.

There was a couple getting into a car that looked expensive. It looked like a Lexus. They looked happy.

"Do you think some people escape pain? Do you think some people get to be happy all their lives?" I asked.

I watched as the man helped the woman into their car, and then he leaned in to give a kiss to her upturned face.

"Oh, I don't know. Maybe there is someone out there—or somebody. I haven't ever met such a person, but then, I probably won't, will I?"

I laughed.

"No, probably not in your line of work."

The Gatekeeper

"Who is this?"

"The gatekeeper."

"Who is she?"

"She decides who comes out. You know, who for which situation—at home, the mother, at work, or the professional—like that."

"But is she you?"

"No," I said and pointed to another picture.

"Oh," she said, "I see."

The Woman

The woman in the picture was soft but looked sad. Her shoulders sagged slightly and she had a timid, fearful look about her as if she dreaded—even anticipated—the next awful thing. She was also beautiful and real. I could see no empty spaces in her eyes. She had a strength that was compelling, and an empathy that I understood.

I realized that I had been trying to make her something strong and forceful, indomitable and able to withstand any storm; strong in the way the world says to be strong—tough, unaffected, and uncaring. However, she wore her weariness and her sufferings calmly and genuinely. She did not seem to think she needed to conquer them. She lived with them. She looked capable of great love.

The Girl

"I think she will talk to us now," I said.

"Really, do you think so?" she asked.

"Yeah," I said, looking out the window again.

Only this time there was no happy couple getting into an expensive car; only black asphalt and the green dumpster at the back of the parking lot.

"Sometimes it helps if you sit in another chair," she suggested.

I shook my head 'no.'

"Okay, then, whenever you're ready."

The girl did not cry as I thought she might. Instead, her voice was steady, and straightforward. Her language was simple, sparse, and clean. She preferred the expressions of the heart and the spirit to the thoughts of the world. In it, I could hear the silence of water, and the strength of mountains. It was a good voice, pleasant and soft, yet strong like the winds that came just before the thunder.

She said, "I wanted to keep my baby. I thought we would have been okay."

Just that…and nothing else. It was all she needed to say. Her words were finally spoken, and heard by someone at last.

The woman with three names said, "I know you did, and I think you would have been fine."

The girl smiled at her and shook her head 'yes.'

The Language and Imagery of a Pilgrim

"And now?" she asked.

I laughed and showed her more pictures.

"Oh my," she said, smiling.

These new pictures would serve as my road map. I could look at them when I got confused and unsure of where I was going. I could stop to examine where to go next, and what I should do next. I would use them to find my way, and as always, I would look for the water.

There were sails flying, elephants running, tigers prowling, zebras playing, so many flowers, colorful boats lined up in a row, windows open, breezes blowing, colored pencils sharpened to a piercing point, a woman sitting at a desk with sunlight flooding her from a nearby window, water washing over beautiful bodies, dancers dancing, food to be eaten, hands reaching out to hands, children running, mothers playing with them, silent beaches, deep waters, beds not made, bridges crossing flat water, porch chairs in a circle, and sunshine on the face of a small girl. The pictures invited you to sit for awhile, or run and play, or sail a boat out into open waters, or laugh, or to sleep peacefully by a window with a breeze, or to swim.

They were the colors of a place where mountains and water come together. They were the colors of islands, of gardens, of children, of blue houses and starry nights. They were beautiful to see.

Colors

I was swimming again. Colors tumbled into my world like waves of soft melting yellows, greens and blues, brilliant oranges, purple and hazy gold, and dusty browns. I went about my days while wave-after-wave of color came back into my world. Stroke-by-stroke, it painted the black canvas that the Tsunami wave had left behind—bringing light into my darkness.

There also was music—beautiful voices singing. I felt alive and joyful, like there was no hole so black or deep in the universe that this music could not fill. The voices were clear and pristine, like winter's icy blue sky. They were the perfect pitch of purity. It was the music of the mountains. It was the color of my home. It was my lake.

I was suddenly amazed at what my life was becoming. I marveled at the changes and the gifts, all so precious to me. I had a blue house with a garden, a child that was so many colors—like a kaleidoscope changing into something more vibrant, and more wonderful each time you looked—and slowly, but maybe, just maybe, love.

Love

"Do you love him?" my mother asked.

I didn't hesitate. "With all my heart," I said, "with all my heart."

"Well," she said, "that's good because that's what it will take, all of it."

I sensed the happiness in her words but there was a warning there, too.

"Now," she said, "you better get out there and rescue him before your father kills him trying to teach him how to ski."

I ran out the door toward the pier.

I waved at them and yelled, "Wait!"

They waved back and slowed the boat down. When I reached the end of the pier, I dove into the water, and soared through the air for what seemed like a lifetime, before feeling the water part and the depths surrounding me.

As I swam toward the boat, I heard my father say, "Now watch, Ivy, and you'll learn something. Ivy, she could always swim."

I would like to say thank you to those who helped me.

First, to Robin Smith, a kind and constant friend who has supported this odd little book—and me—unfailingly through many years. Thank you.

To Bess Arendall, a talented young woman with vision and grace, who saw the pictures and story as one, and did an awesome job designing the lay-out of this book. Your efforts were tireless, patient, and a job well-done. Thank you.

To my husband, Marvin Bagwell, I always told you that if I ever got anything published I would say I had done it in spite of you! Well, too true, but in the end, you have believed in me more than I have believed in myself. You are my treasure and my rock. You have supported me with hours of listening to what did not make sense to you, while providing me with the very place to write. You even gave me my own "Upper Room." I love you. Thank you for being my husband and my friend.

To my children, Joffrey and Micah Bagwell, who sacrificed a trip to Disney World for this book, thank you. Joffrey you have an artist's soul and a heart for the wounded, you will serve this world well. Thank you for letting me see this book through your eyes. Micah, you are brave and true, a soldier in heart and spirit—a real protector. Your words still ring in my ears, "If you want to write, Mommy, write." You are both too cool. Thank you!

To Adam Bennett, a young man of faith and knowledge, I am so thankful for the thousand e-mails and the thousand times thousand help you gave me. This love/hate relationship with my computer is only working because of you. Thank you for using your talents to serve our Lord.

To June Groh, Susan Huranna, Marge Hansel, Nancy Nesbitt, Karen Doucette, and Sheila Schutt—women with a passion for Christ and a willingness to go out on a limb for him—you are phenomenal women of faith and your support is huge in my life. My gratitude and my love, I extend to each of you.

And last, to Jeanine Siler Jones, thank you.

To God be all Glory and Praise,

Cinthia